Daily Moments with God

In Quietness and Confidence

Jacqueline E. McCullough

D0770050

Daily Moments with God

In Quietness and Confidence

Jacqueline E. McCullough

Pneuma Life Publishing
P. O. Box 1127
Rockville, MD 20849
(301) 251-4470
(800) 727-3218

1/96

Contents

Dedication

This book is dedicated to my loving, caring and Spirit-filled parents, Reverend Percival and Evangelist Keturah Phillips; my sister, Rose Woody; my brother, Charles Dwayne Phillips; and my extended family who has always supported my efforts to please the Lord.

Acknowledgments

A special thanks to my pastor, Bishop W.S. McKinley, who has been a tremendous source of inspiration, guidance and instruction, and to the Elim International Church, which has been a place of strength, healing and deliverance.

I would also like to thank my dear friends and prayer partners, especially Dr. Carolyn D. Showell and Professor Gail Ann Hightower, for their undaunting support and positive response to this endeavor.

A very special thanks to Gerre Samuels (Editor), Gwen Campbell (Daughters of Rizpah Administrator) and the Daughters of Rizpah Staff for making the preparation of this project possible.

Foreword

Today, more than ever, we must steal away from our hurried lives to be with Jesus. Daily we must reaffirm our commitment to glorify Him in thought, word and deed. God uses the undulation of our emotions — our mountaintop and valley experiences — to prevent us from being lulled into passivity and dulled by inactivity.

Reverend Jacqueline E. McCullough has poignantly revealed the heart of Him Who first loved us. Amidst the confusion of the world, she implores us to surrender all of ourselves so that we may know the peace and joy that the Lord longs to bequeath us.

In Quietness and Confidence arrests our emotions and challenges our minds. When we struggle with indecisiveness, doubt, fear, mistrust and the immobility that springs from guilt, we need to return to the One who "spared not His own Son" and desires to "freely give us all things" (Romans 8:32). These writings point us to the only source of stability, faith, love and confidence in this life.

We can refuse to return to the past. We are new in Jesus Christ. He made us; therefore, He made a way of escape for us who continue to "press toward the mark for the prize of the high calling of God in Christ Jesus" (Philippians 3:14).

I pray that you make this devotional a companion to your daily Bible reading. May you know the victory that is yours because of Him Who went before you.

Gerre Samuels
Brooklyn, New York

Introduction

This book presents a unique exposition of poetry, punctuated phrases and sermonettes. This creative, inspired and thought-provoking blend centers on the theme of trusting, believing, loving and obeying the Lord Jesus Christ.

These writings create a forum for the reader to express reflections, passions, prayers, praise and worship to God concerning situations of daily life. This book does not offer comprehensive answers to one's dilemmas and problems, but it will motivate the reader to develop freedom and openness in his or her communication with the Lord.

The poems aspire to enchant the reader's spiritual and emotional ear. In turn, a new level of introspection, honesty, confession, change and intimacy will be engendered. These creative compositions appeal to the imaginative mind and spiritually impressionable soul.

The thoughts or phrases that follow condense the theme of each poem. This nutshell-like idiom will attach itself to the perception of those who require a quick word for the day or who readily respond to lively or spirited proverbs.

The Bible verses and sermonettes, which appeal to the studious or inquisitive mind, offer a contextual focus and a pointed, functional application. For those who are given to research and examination of the Scriptures, it may incite them to greater illumination of the passage, which will reveal a wealth of knowledge and take the reader on a journey from sermonettes to sermons to messages and, perhaps, to rhemas.

In Quietness and Confidence, a daily meditation, will usher one into a new place of stillness, attentiveness and rest where God desires to impart confidence, security and balance.

May those whose hearts are bereft of the "peace which passeth all understanding" (Philippians 4:7) find wonderful consolation in Jesus Christ.

In Quietness and Confidence

My heart pounding;
My eyes blinking;
My thoughts wandering;
My soul disquieting.

Shadows and images floating in the dark;
Life seems to stand still
and time has no start.

Where am I, and how do I move?
Looking for answers, searching for truth.
My anxiety is now heightened;
My fears have become strong.

Hopelessness and despair have driven
away my song.
Hush, night! Calm you, my spirit!
I hear a still voice penetrating my fright.

It is a familiar voice I hear.
A tone so soft and tender to the ear.
Jesus, my Master, has drawn so very near.
His words dispel the gloom and calm my fear.

All is well; the place is free from ill.
Jesus has come to teach me how to be still.

The Stillness of Silence

"For thus saith the Lord God, the Holy One of Israel; In returning and rest shall ye be saved; in quietness and in confidence shall be your strength: and ye would not." Isaiah 30:15

This scripture focuses on Israel's trust and reliance on Egypt rather than having confidence in God. King Hezekiah followed the foolish counsel of secretly aligning Israel with Egypt instead of trusting God to deliver them against the oppression of the Assyrians. The prophets of God warned Israel to "return to him," which means to repent, to break, to cease and to bring again. They were also to rest (to lean on, to trust or to rely on); to have quietness (to be still, to settle, to be appeased); to have confidence (to trust, to be assured, secured, hopeful).

The reward for rest was salvation (to be free, to be succored, to be rescued). The recompense for quietness and confidence was strength (valor, victory, might). Yet, they rejected these spiritual and emotional graces to depend on the Egyptian army.

Will you trust God in quietness and confidence for the most difficult area of your life, or will you forfeit victory for the obvious or apparent? Trust God!

Crushed to Sweetness

Excitement at its peak,
Movement swift and sure,
Heart throbs loud and strong,
But I am found hopelessly in the wrong.

This plan of mine, so clear,
Glided along without doubt and fear.
Suddenly, with a great blast,
Apprehension seizes me fast.

My world is being demolished
Before my very eyes.
Confidence in the future is eroding
And promises seem far beyond the skies.

Thought this road I chose
Would be free from sorrow or pain.
But time has taught me differently
And much wisdom I have gained.

Pride and false security were squeezed
And pulled from my will.
I watched my ambitions escape
To obscurity hill.

In the midst of it I encountered
The Rose of Sharon Himself.
His sweet scent I have found
And His tender touch I have felt.

His aroma soothes and bathes me
In the fragrance of His grace.
This presence engulfs me and
Removes life's bitter taste.

The experience is so awesome.
It forces others to see how bitterness and sorrow
Can be transformed into the sweet tomorrow.

Spiritual Aromatic Aura

"But he was wounded for our transgressions, he was bruised for our iniquities: the chastisement of our peace was upon him; and with his stripes we are healed." Isaiah 53:5

The prophet vividly portrayed Jesus' suffering and humiliation in this chapter. Yet, through His humiliation, He became our victor and conquering king. This verse describes the intensity of His anguish and the power of His redemption.

A full characterization of Jesus' agony can be explained by the key words in the text: He was wounded (broken, slain or stained) for our transgressions (rebellion, revolt and trespasses); He was bruised (to crush, to smite), for our iniquities (faults, perversities); the chastisement of our peace (the punishment brings about our peace, safety, health, prosperity) was upon Him; with His stripes (black and blue marks, bruises, wounds) we are healed (cured, made whole, mended).

Knowing this, we should be consciously aware of the price Jesus paid to bring about healing, salvation and deliverance. His death enables us to possess beauty, tranquility and innumerable blessings.

Jesus is our perfect example of the act of humility(crushing) becoming the place of victory (sweetness and beauty).

Mountain Climber

Satisfied and rested in a place that
was not strange. Yet, it is losing its fancy
because of the aura of change. Knowing times and
seasons, shifts and tides of life, prepares me for
larger steps and gigantic strides.

The mountain now awaits me. The challenge echoes
its call. Come up higher in your spirit and view
the great and tall.

Limitless dreams and boundless visions
direct my paths and guard my decisions.
God's treasures are in the mountains.
The streams are flowing from higher fountains.

Rise High, Mountain Climber!

*"Now therefore give me this mountain, whereof the Lord spake in that day;
for thou heardest in that day how the Anakims were there, and that the cities
were great and fenced: if so be the Lord will be with me, then I shall be able
to drive them out, as the Lord said." Joshua 14:12*

The inheritance of each tribe was determined by lot (Numbers 34:16-29).
Out of the twelve spies who viewed Canaan, only Caleb and Joshua brought
back a good report. Caleb encouraged the people, "Let us go up at once, and
possess it; for we are well able to overcome it" (Numbers 13:30). Now eighty-
five years old, Caleb came to Joshua in the true nature of his name (dog,
impetuous) and asked for a specific portion of land that Moses had given him
forty-five years earlier (Numbers 14:24,30; Deut. 1:36).

This land was filled with Anakims — giants (meaning to choke, to strangulate,
to chain). Though he was much older, Caleb felt he was well able to handle
this challenge with the same tenacity and power as when he was younger.

Your mountains are awaiting the impetuous and dynamic freedom of the
Holy Spirit in your life, which will enable you to reach your highest potential.

Loved into Love

Losing control, choosing not to hate,
touching without fear came from God's
grace, which He freely shared.

Guarding my emotions was the name of
the game. Giving with a price was protection
against shame. I couldn't resist the power of
God's presence. The freedom of His love lured me
into a new spiritual residence.

Yes, to live in a realm of awareness of God's
care engulfs the spirit and summons one to hear.
I felt pain, but I experienced His balm.
I saw my lowliness, but He issued confidence
and calm.

His lessons are revealing and He ministers
unending healing. My purpose in life was nobler
than a call. He taught me to receive the
greatest gift of all — love.

A Love Lift

"Though I speak with the tongues of men and of angels, and have not charity,
I am become as sounding brass, or a tinkling cymbal." 1 Corinthians 13:1

Paul, the outstanding New Testament apostle and teacher, repeatedly instructed the church at Corinth regarding a proper balance between spiritual gifts and character. He defines and outlines spiritual gifts and their functions in the Body of Christ (1 Cor. 12). He closes this chapter, however, by exhorting them to follow "a more excellent way" of relating beyond the contribution of one's gift in the church.

All spiritual gifts must be couched in love if they are to minister life. If one can speak all languages and even understand angelic communication but does not have love (agape —godly, committed love), then that person is like a clanging gong or cymbal. Though he may make a lot of noise or attract attention to himself, his life is empty and hollow. Your Christian life is not evaluated merely by your skill or giftedness but by the depth of your character to love, respect, honor and touch another person's heart.

Yes, it's exciting to be used by God, but you should also desire godly character. Learn to love and you will walk in "a more excellent way."

Feeling Free

Barriers are removed, hedges torn down.
I'm lifted from low valleys, loosed,
delivered, not bound.

Lightheartedness embraces, surrounded
by a song. With God's mighty wings under-
girding, I'm soaring far and long.

Chainless, limitless, tireless describe
my destiny. Time and period pass, and age has
become a friend, at last.

Winged arms, unshackled feet, glorious
calm, no defeat. Feeling free!

Wings in Flight

"If the Son therefore shall make you free, ye shall be free indeed."
John 8:36

This chapter clearly represents Jesus' earthly teaching ministry. The portion of this chapter that applies to this meditation emphasizes discipleship. His challenge to commitment was centered on acknowledging and accepting His mission and purpose on earth.

Anyone who believes that Jesus is the Messiah and Savior — and continues to walk in His ways — will know (understand) the truth (doctrine), which will make free (liberate) that person.

We think freedom is acting independently of God and avoiding any demands of discipleship to Jesus Christ. Yet, the Scriptures declare that when we submit to His Lordship and obey Him, we will experience true freedom and a fulfilled life.

Glorious Possibilities

Chance and luck are words of the past.
Experience has taught me that prosperity
seldom comes quickly or fast.

The world pushes and urges one to gamble
and to bet. Many have destroyed themselves
and haven't gotten rich yet.

God's plan for wealth goes far beyond the
money. His richness of life is sweeter than
honey. Inspiration, creativity, perception and
grace go way beyond the dollar and moves me up
life's ladder.

The notion of greater horizons, old doors
becoming new, excites my enthusiasm and
makes my dreams come true. Defeat creates
stepping stones and mistakes emerge as my
teacher. Burdens gave me insight and sorrows
scented me sweeter.

Days are meaningful, nights are luminous.
Tomorrows are promising because possibilities
are flourishing.

Inundated With Hope

"But Jesus beheld them, and said unto them, With men this is impossible; but with God all things are possible." Matthew 19:26

Jesus' encounter with the rich young ruler preceded this verse. The man was probably too young to be a member of the Sanhedrin but perhaps came from a very rich and prominent family.

He came to Jesus and asked, "Good Master, what good thing shall I do, that I may have eternal life?" (Matthew 19:16) Jesus questioned the young man's concept of "good," saying that no one was good but God alone. The young man claimed to have observed all the obvious commandments. Knowing his idea of goodness was based on his outward, ritualistic observance of the Law, Jesus challenged him to genuine conversion. "Go and sell that thou hast, and give to the poor, and thou shalt have treasure in heaven: and come and follow me" (Matthew 19:21). Finding this command too difficult to fulfill, the young man went away sorrowful for he had many possessions.

Jesus declared, "It is easier for a camel to go through the eye of a needle, than for a rich man to enter into the kingdom of God" (Matthew 19:24). When a man becomes enthralled with earthly possessions, it is very difficult for him to embrace the committed, sacrificial life of a believer.

"Then who can be saved?" the disciples wanted to know. Jesus said, "With men this is impossible; but with God all things are possible." Only God can enable us to live this kind of life. His grace does not come solely by religious observances but by the power of Jesus in the life of the believer.

Jesus also confronts you with denial of self, submission and His call to discipleship. Will you also walk away or will you say yes to Him?

Me in Touch with Me

The mirrored image I now view, appears
estranged from what I knew.
The lines pronounced around my mouth
recall expressions of smiles and pouts.

Swings of emotions without definition,
wrinkled brows with pain and confusion,
broken heart hidden behind a broad chest
created a system of survival and stress.

Culture, family and religion taught me to
mask genuine emotion. It took God to
expose all the lies and to flood me with
honesty, which led me to true devotion.

His steadfast love removed my cover and
embraced me with enormous power. Perfection has not
been achieved, but awareness resides eternally deep.
My love for God demands intimacy and truth;
removal of deception always follows suit.

Oh, what relief awaits me when I accept who I am.
With the light of Jesus flowing, I can surely
stand. Anger, I know you and why you linger there.
Fear, you are no stranger, and I see the clothes
you wear. Insecurity forces me to compete and always
in vain. Yet, love, you have embraced me with passion
untamed. I am in touch with the me that was lost
and the me I must gain.

Me Touching Me in the Midst of God Holding Me

"But by the grace of God I am what I am." 1 Corinthians 15:10

The Apostle Paul presents this eloquent defense of the authenticity of the resurrection of Jesus Christ. Eyewitnesses of the resurrected Christ included Peter, the Twelve, the Five Hundred, James and then all the Apostles. Paul also claimed that he himself saw the Lord.

Once an enemy of the Church, Paul now claimed to be a bonafide witness of the resurrected Christ, which was one of the criteria for affirming one's apostleship.

This argument confirmed that he was not part of the original Twelve but among the least of the apostles because of his past. He describes his apostleship as one born out of due time (an aborted fetus that lived). He was not supposed to be included, but God's grace (favor) converted him, secured him, empowered him and placed him in the hierarchy of the church.

Paul was thoroughly aware of his faults and weaknesses, but he was also clearly cognizant of what he had become in God. Are you in touch with yourself and gloriously excited about the you that is growing through the grace of God? You should be!

Waiting Beyond the Wait

How far must I go before I can stop?
How high must I climb to reach the top?
How much should I give in order to gain?
How do I say no to the lingering pain?

My mind shouts for change.
My spirit echoes, "No delay."
My doubt and confusion cry out,
"No way."

I know God's Word and promises are true.
I know that His presence overshadows
as the morning dew.
I know of the victories of the past.
I know, in spite of the wait,
that He will deliver at last.

Every day I draw closer.
Each time I learn more.
Something was not ready;
Someone was not quite sure.

If it had happened yesterday,
All would not be well.
If the door was open earlier,
I would have stumbled and fell.
If the prize was given sooner,
Then pride would rise and swell.

Wisdom caught my weary heart.
Knowledge kept me from falling apart.
Praise God, who soothes my anxious spirit.
Grace and peace covered me in it.

I Have Traveled Beyond the Wait

"Wherefore take unto you the whole armour of God, that ye may be able to withstand in the evil day, and having done all, to stand. Stand therefore . . . ." Ephesians 6:13,14a

Ephesians 6:10-18 talks about warfare. Christians may struggle with the daily difficulties of life, but we're also engaged in conflict with the powers of darkness.

The believer must be well-armed, equipped and fortified to handle this battle. We often stress the armor of the Word, prayer, praise and fasting. The ability to stand, however, is also a part of one's defense against the wiles of the enemy.

The adversary is determined to undermine our faith in God. He wants us to cast away our confidence in God's Word. He wants us to forget all that God had done in our lives. Our stressful, wearisome times attract the attention of the enemy and his cohorts. Especially during these times, we must stand (abide, resist, oppose, hold up, establish). When we have done all we can, then we must stand our ground and resist.

Our faith is constantly being tested and tried by our opponent, but part of our defense and victory is to be stable in the knowledge of the Lord Jesus Christ. Stand and stand again!

Another Praise

When praise meets praise, and song
mingles with song, then time is no
obstacle and foe can't restrain the
throng.

Overwhelming warmth of comfort,
Intense desire to get close,
The Creator draws nigh and His Spirit
lifts us high.

Weariness, however, causes my lips to be
parched and dry. My arms become heavy
and I lose my will to try.

Is it that I don't love Him?
How could I cease to praise?
My Life, Joy and Savior should be the
words I raise.

This act must be continuously done,
and I must bless Him with my tongue.
Only a gift of sacrifice will honorably
suffice. God demands and must receive praises,
for it is He who takes me through my phases.

Well, it took many years to master
this, to know the depth of praise
beyond the abyss. The lessons from
the throne have clearly defined the
power of praise and the ecstasy of
spiritual bliss.

I Will Give Him Another Praise

"By him therefore let us offer the sacrifice of praise to God continually, that is, the fruit of our lips giving thanks to his name." Hebrews 13:15

This writer challenged the Hebrew believers to godly character and life-style. He then accentuated the perfect sacrifice that Jesus proffered on our behalf.

He suffered shame, reproach and abandonment through His propitious death on Calvary. With this in mind, we are encouraged to make a continuous oblation of praise to God.

The altar of our hearts has replaced the altar of stone in the priestly order of animal sacrifice in the Old Testament. Jesus became our supreme offering; therefore, we must take on this attitude by giving Him what He requires.

The sacrifice of praise connotes the believer becoming an altar, not of blood, but of praise (thanksgiving) to God continually, under all circumstances. This is demonstrated or expressed through the fruit of our lips (literally by plucking or pulling out) giving thanks (to acknowledge, to confess) to His name (talking about His character). The lips are a place of pouring out, which indicates a free, flowing expression without restraint or hesitation.

This praise flows from the heart and mouth of those who realize that Jesus paid it all, and all to Him we owe.

Long Way — Shortcut

Conserving energy, saving time,
circumventing the obstacles in my haste
to shine gave me a false sense of control.
I tried to rush my progress, but
neglected my soul.

Now, the lessons that I learned taught me
to work timely to the end. My pace and
my purpose no longer fold or bend.

Manipulation and ingenuity were my
calling cards. Networking and profiling
became the maps and charts. I created and
wove a finished piece, yet, the blends were
separating and the mixes had no peace.

No more pats on the back, dear ego.
You missed some needed truths. Go back to the
beginning and settle into God's grove.
The trails and paths were blazed by Him.
The guiding light will subdue the dim.

Haste not, nor skip to move ahead.
Too many pitfalls lie as flower beds.
The shortcuts turn to a wandering journey
and will lead one to fumble and scurry.

This march follows the rhythm
of the drum that beats out of heaven.
This pounding pulse can only be heard
by those who yield to God as the bread
that is unleavened.

God's path is longer but brighter and
fairer. It is the shortcut that brings
one nearer.

An Arrowed Path

"But he knoweth the way that I take: when he hath tried me, I shall come forth as gold." Job 23:10

Job had become weary in his affliction and suffering. Unable to see or hear from God concerning his plight, Job languished. He just wanted an answer and direction from the mouth of God.

Job concluded that even if God is hidden from his view, he is not hidden from God. God had ordered his steps. Although his life was in total chaos, God was still directing his life.

"He [God] knoweth the way that I take." This means God appointed, acknowledged, advised the way (conversation, custom, journey, manner) that Job took. "When he [God] hath tried me, I shall come forth as gold." When God has tested, proven and examined me, with luster I shall bring forth and break out as clear sky and fair weather.

This path that God has chosen will ultimately bring you to your place of clarity and destiny.

The Finish

Hour by hour I wait for the finish.
The end is in view and this attack
has a limit. My tears have all vanished.
My heart pants subsided.

"Persevere!" my soul cries. The finale will
bring the prize. Push, stretch, reach
and touch the end. Your victory is sure
and your future will not suspend.

This is the moment of delivery and birth.
This is the era of maturity and growth.
God has fulfilled His providence and care.
The bitter sweet cup of defeat and victory
I share.

The Start and Finish Have Now Become One

"Know ye not that they which run in a race run all, but one receiveth the prize? So run, that ye may obtain." 1 Corinthians 9:24

This entire chapter of Scripture expresses the great defense that the Apostle Paul heaved at the Corinthian church as they questioned his apostleship and his right to be supported financially in the ministry.

Paul refrained from demanding his right to be adequately rewarded for his labor. Because of their carnality toward spiritual things, Paul forfeited his pastoral benefits to prove he could give up his rights for the kingdom. He adjusted to any situation to prove his commitment to God.

Willing to forsake anything so the gospel will be received, Paul then challenged them to run the race without hesitation. A glorious crown of righteousness awaits believers at the finish line.

In other words, be aware, take note that anyone who runs (approaches a course) must do the whole, that he or she may attain the prize (award). I command you to finish your course so that you may possess the reward assigned to you.

Power to Receive

Willingly and freely I give with a smile.
Holding goodies and nuggets for the old
ones and the child.

Oh, what joy they give me when I bless them
with things. I enjoy donating and sharing
because it propels my wings.

I feel a sense of purity and goodness
in my mind. I have conformed to Scripture
and that is truly divine.

Yet, my struggles begin when they turn
and say, "It's your turn to get, so let me
make your day." Well, disarmed is just a
mild description of my emotional dismay.
It is so much easier to give and just
walk away.

I often gave, expecting to receive in
return, but only to be thwarted and
spurned. I kept on giving without
reward and forgot that reaping was
a proper award.

Grace to receive all the blessings
that are assured is a constant prayer.
I will not allow pride and power to keep
me from being an inheritor.

Lord, help me to accept the humility of getting.
I will smile and shout with joy because
I have yielded to the modesty of receiving.

Embracing Life's Favors

"Give, and it shall be given unto you; good measure, pressed down, and shaken together, and running over, shall men give into your bosom. For with the same measure that ye mete withal it shall be measured to you again."

Luke 6:38

Jesus had just chosen the Twelve, the disciples whom He would train during the next two and a half years with His teachings, demonstrations of power and experiences.

Jesus taught His kingdom principles to the Twelve (verses 20-49). Being a king, Jesus looked for subjects to live in His kingdom. To enter and live in this kingdom, one has to be taught.

This lesson deals with proper attitudes toward fellow Christians. We should not judge or condemn, but we should forgive and also give. This giving is not limited to friends but also to enemies.

The gift of giving brings the reward of receiving. "Give and it shall be given unto you." Give (bestow, grant, offer or minister) and it shall be given (bestowed, offered and ministered) unto you. Good measure (proper portion or degree), pressed down (squeezed down or packed down), shaken together (agitated or stirred up), running over (overflowing beyond capacity) shall men give into your bosom (bay, creek, brook, stream). For with the same portion you allot, it shall be returned unto you.

Can you visualize the system God has established to bless you? Open up your spirit and appropriate your godly returns.

Growing into Maturity

Some teddy bears are packed away,
Few ribbons are still on display,
Dolls and trains peep from their corners
To remind me that the child is still
lingering at my borders.

It's all right to be childlike and float
with a carefree spirit. The conflict
is the childishness that goes along with it.

The naive disposition, which seeks to be impressed
with life and things is its greatest quest.
Jesus demanded a trusting outlook from
His students on earth. This attitude that brings
power and new birth.

Childishness, however, halts the progress
and the move. Its limits are apparent
and its performance can be crude.
Insecurities, selfishness, arrogance and
pride are the result of an adult behaving
as a child.

Fighting petty battles, losing major wars,
hurting those we love and always trying
to score. Refusing to forgive, inflexible
in thought, wounded in spirit and very
easily bought are just some of the
struggles that immaturity brings to the
hearts of those who will not let Jesus
play His part.

Rise up, oh foolish heart,
help is on the way.
Life's lectures must be taught
and a willing heart must obey.
Embrace the growing pains and
reach for the One who reigns.
You will find that sweet embrace
as you stick to the maturing pace.

From Growth to Maturity

"But we all, with open face beholding as in a glass the glory of the Lord, are changed into the same image from glory to glory, even as by the Spirit of the Lord." 2 Corinthians 3:18

This scriptural text notes Paul's commendation of his ministry and apostleship. He wanted the Corinthians to assess quality ministry and quality life in Jesus Christ by viewing spiritual relationship through his eyes. He cherishes the New Testament covenant because it is superior to the Old Testament.

Moses' account in Exodus 34:29-35 shows us the effects of closeness with God and how it affected his countenance. Paul emphasizes the benefits of this relationship, which leads one into transformation and maturity.

These benefits include liberty. God's presence is not veiled from us or exclusive to the high priest but open to all who believe in Him. In this liberty we have intimacy (closeness) as we behold Him in His splendor and awesomeness (Exodus 33:17-23; 1 John 3:1,2). In this place of openness to the Lord, one is transformed (changed into His image) from glory to glory by the Spirit of the Lord.

Let us yield to the Spirit in the presence of the Lord while we worship freely and imbibe in true intimacy. As a result, we will be changed, blessed and made honorable in the sight of God, which is true maturity.

A Repairer of Breaches

The bridge is burnt, the cord is broken.
The touch is gone, the sound forgotten.
There is no speech, the body dangles limp.
The eyes stare in space and the
spirits make no link.

There must be a way to heal this brokenness.
There must be a time that we connect breast
to breast. There are still words that will spawn
new life. I must be the one to extend
without strife.

God will give me the power to piece this
difficult puzzle. I will not be defeated
or give up the struggle.

Connect the line, bring up the wood,
retwine the cord and make this moment
good. Time to fix, time to heal,
time to bind up and time to be real.

Mended Into Wholeness

"And they that shall be of thee shall build the old waste places: thou shalt raise up the foundations of many generations; and thou shalt be called, The repairer of the breach, The restorer of paths to dwell in." Isaiah 58:12

The Jews in Isaiah's time were entrenched in an outward show of worship with little or no commitment to inward holiness. Some scholars say this passage describes the Jews in exile when they could not practice their religion but could fast and pray for deliverance.

The issue here is not the validity of fasting but the motive of fasting. Israel engaged in hypocritical worship and devotion. Thus, God encouraged them to repent. As a result, they would be restored and their future would be promising.

Verse 12 recounts some of the promises of the post-exilic period to a holy people. They would build the places that had been torn down or ruined. They would lay the foundation of the temple for future generations to worship. They would also repair or mend the wickedness of their wrong doings and restore the standards, reconstructing a godly, safe and righteous community.

Let us be menders and healers of a broken, ungodly and hypocritical society that performs religious rites but lacks Christian character.

Inspired Creativity

Obscured annoyance and passive compliance
describe my demeanor and my performance.
One day I read from the Holy Writ a passage
that grabbed me and gave me spiritual wit.

"I have put my words in thy mouth,
and I have covered thee in the shadow
of mine hand, that I may plant the heavens,
and lay the foundations of the earth,
and say unto Zion, Thou art my people."
Isaiah 51:16

I went from day to day seeking my place.
Nights echoed with mocking, thoughts
of ruin and waste.

I prayed, worshiped, studied and cried,
but my head was drenched with sorrow and my
creativity died. Suddenly I arose with discerning
in my thoughts. I saw deliverance and I snatched
a new start.

I begot songs in my soul and melodies upon my
ear. Words effused from my lips and charged the
atmosphere.

My pen became swift with phrases so unique. The
hidden virtues emerged and I was no longer weak.
My utterances are alive and free. My tongue
quickens with fiery speech.

The power to create has been illumined by the
Great, the One who issues life to the spirit that
will wait.

I Am Wholly Creative

One can find encouragement as Israel probably did during the Babylonian exile. The prophet encouraged them to trust in the Lord for their deliverance even though they were in a difficult place.

Isaiah 51:16 expresses God's determination to restore and empower His people during such a perplexing time of captivity. He promised to put His words (counsel, law, commandment, eloquence, language and power) in their mouths (mind and speech).

He also promised to cover (conceal, hide and clothe) them in His hand or by His power. The fulfillment of this promise would unveil and establish His purpose in the heavens and in the nation of Israel.

This demonstration of His steadfast love proclaimed to the universe that God is with His people. This would be reflected in their ability to be inspired by His Word and to adhere to His commandment. This is the soil from which creativity emerges and inspiration arises. The more we partake of His Word, the more the Holy Spirit is able to release our inventive capabilities.

> *"The statues of the Lord are right,*
> *rejoicing the heart: the commandment*
> *of the Lord is pure, enlightening the eyes....*
> *More to be desired are they than gold, yea,*
> *than much fine gold: sweeter also than honey*
> *and the honeycomb."*
>
> *Psalm 19:8,10*

The Honor of Marriage

Sobered to think one should seek to bind his
heart to mine. Happy to know that loneliness will
cease to torment my mind.

I wonder what caused us to secure this bond
around this matrimony of love that soars beyond.
The lust is over, the passion has gone dry.
The years have passed, and drudgery lingers by.

Yet, there is an abiding sense of belonging,
respect and dignity that keep our hearts
throbbing. Honor is the key that opens
the way to trust, which is hard to find among the
emotional floods of lust.

When our vows were exchanged, we did not
understand that loving and caring are more
than a wedding band. Humbled to receive
your confidence and care, your sorrow
and weakness, your shame and despair.

The Bible states that your body is mine.
I treasure and guard it even though it
ages with time. I honor and esteem you,
even the comely signs, because I realize
this thing that we have is truly divine.

It was the chance of life that we both
espoused. Determination and conviction
helped to keep our sacred house. You are
deserving of my life, time and strength.
We did not refrain from spiritual grace and
emotional health. The honor of our marriage is the
seal that guards the reins to the sacredness of
our intimacy and has lessened life pains.

I Pay Tribute to Our Union

"Marriage is honourable in all, and the bed undefiled: but whoremongers and adulterers God will judge." Hebrews 13:4

Our Christianity is readily seen in our relationship with other people, namely, our family. This verse touches the most primary, intimate and God-ordained connection: marriage.

This scripture was written perhaps to a church in Rome or to some of the cities of the Mediterranean East whose society disregarded the honor, fidelity and chastity of marriage. The writer hurled a challenge to a Christian approach and appreciation for this sacred union, which should be guarded and nurtured by God's available grace. Others promoted celibacy and asceticism (reclusiveness) as the supreme antidote to immorality, adultery, fornication and perversion.

Even though many will not unite in holy matrimony, one must recognize God's ideal plan for a wholesome life, healthy socialization, powerful spirituality and fruitful reproduction. This is truly found in an honorable union that does not rob, defile or spoil the bliss, intimacy, oneness, tenderness and exclusiveness of the marital bed.

Oh, that we would look at this glorious institution, which is constantly under diabolical attack. Hopefully, we will begin to see the beauty, security and healthy benefits to be derived from this commitment to oneness and loyalty.

Facing the Worst

Inventing fears before they are warranted,
crying tears and hastily feeling cheated.
This is how a coward spends life and how a
loser lives inside.

Engaging in battles that are won, asking
for allies when the enemy is gone.
Living afraid of fear itself and
walking in shadows of the dead.

Well, just imagine the worst the world
can bring, whether death, sickness or
some horrible thing. Face it! Look at it!
Feel it! Hold it! Let sorrow and
its darkness overshadow your spirit.
Let grief and pain linger for a minute.

Examine your loss, bear the heavy cross.
Cry the burning tear and tremble with fear.
Then when you meet the worst that could
ever be, look at yourself and you will
clearly see.

God's grace took you through the drama of it all.
He hoisted your feet and made you soar without a
fall. The giant problem has been reduced to an
ant. You can face the harshest by destroying
your can't.

I Handled It

"Yea, though I walk through the valley of the shadow of death, I will fear no evil: for thou art with me; thy rod and thy staff they comfort me."
Psalm 23:4

David, the writer of this psalm, understood pastoral life. As a shepherd, he cared for his father's sheep while his older brothers followed King Saul.

David used the metaphor from his years of shepherding to stamp in our hearts the providential care of God — our Jehovah Jireh — which includes invigoration, direction, preservation and prosperity.

With this in mind, David recalled the times when he was found in "the valley of the shadow of death." This describes a ravine (long, hollow gorge or pass formed by torrents or heavy rain) overhung by precipitous cliffs filled with thick forests, which create an aura of danger and destruction. Sheep pass through these life-threatening passages but escape its peril.

Jesus Christ — the Good Shepherd — allays our fear (dread and terror), dispels evil (adversity, affliction and harm), uses His rod (scepter, rulership, power) and staff (support, sustenance) to comfort (console, ease and protect) us.

This is good news to the heart of one who passes through hazardous circumstances. You will come through unharmed because Jesus is the Shepherd and Bishop of your soul.

The Returning Children

God, you remember how I fought for control
of my little ones. The older they grew,
the stronger I held them to my heart and
never wanted them to part.

I sought to protect and keep them from pain.
Danger was hovering and trouble would not
refrain. You tugged at my world and challenged
my will. I listened but was helpless, my
passion lingered still.

Then all at once the children pulled away,
cut the apron strings and called it a day.
Beaten and wounded, I wept bitter and sore.
These idols are gone and life landed me
on a new shore.

They were tossed and driven by the sea
of reality. They rocked and reeled
in the wind of calamity. But I
remembered the nights that I prayed.
I taught them the Word of God, even though they
resisted and swayed. I anointed
them with oil and rebuked the evil force.
I gave them principles that would become
their resource.

I can now relax into the truth of God's
Word. My heart is no longer heavy but
is fully assured. Years later, one by one,
they returned to the Lord. They are battled
scarred and weary, but what a great victory
and reward.

Thank God I released them in the Spirit and the
truth, which preserved and kept them and now
it is a living proof.

Children Will Come Back to God

"Train up a child in the way he should go: and when he is old, he will not depart from it." Proverbs 22:6

Most scholars concur that this book was written by King Solomon, the wisest man who ever lived. A proverb can be described as a profound statement that clearly communicates truth. The Hebrew word for proverb is "mashal," which means comparison. Biblical wisdom literature often teaches by use of comparison, namely, the reward of good and evil, the plight of the wise and foolish and the expected end of the diligent and the slothful.

This proverb highlights the effect of parental training (early instruction) of the child (infancy to adolescence) in the way (purpose, course of life, assignment) he or she should go (appointment, path). When they age, they will not depart (decline, withdraw or revolt) from it.

This promise will pay off to the diligent, teaching and nurturing parent. Even if you are a single parent, God does not exclude you from this blessing. Your child may initially or temporarily stray, but the Word of God will constrain him or her back in "the way."

Godly Defiance

My stumbling block seems unmovable,
my doors are steel and brass. My
chains serve to bind me, and my
life seems withered as grass.

I reach for deliverance, but the press
grows hard and strong. My plight
is not left to chance. God will fix
things that are wrong.

Persistence, defiance and determination
are stirring me to pray. Even though
years have passed and time goes on its way.

I know that the change will come, if I
just keep holding on. Whenever I let go,
Jesus' promises begin to flow.

The shift will come when I least
expect. Not by giving in, but
acting as an elect. Through all
of this, my mind has been filled
with the power of defiance and
the will of persistence.

Overcomer

"And shall not God avenge his own elect, which cry day and night unto him, though he bear long with them?" Luke 18:7

This verse, from the Parable of the Unjust Judge, urges us to pray without ceasing. This woman approached the judge with importunity, which is to entreat pressingly or to insist repeatedly. This unjust, unrighteous and insensitive judge responded to this widow's request to be avenged (vindicated) of her enemy.

Her persistent plea for an audience with this judge resulted in his favorable response. She was determined and defiant to the end.

Jesus noted that if this ungodly judge succumbed to the pressure of stubborn faith, then how much more will God, who loves and cares for His people, respond to those who continue in faithful prayer and supplication to Him? Pray one more prayer.

Windless Seasons

Arid and still, bespeaks of the time.
Moments waiting and hours stand by.
Am I moving or is this a mirage?
Am I viewing my dreams at large?

I breathe the same air.
I think the same thoughts.
I see the same people.
I feel trapped and feeble.

The freshness of newness seems
to cease as the breeze. Someone describes
my life as being squashed and squeezed.

The illusions of oasis in my seared and
listless land have played its tricks
so often and left me buried in the sand.

Oh, how well I recall the cloudless,
windless days. The times of barrenness
and the desert-like paths and ways.

Yet, I feel a light wind blowing from the
east, the place of new beginnings where
the past forgets its defeat.

The dryness will soon be over. I see
the cloud ahead. My God has proven
faithful, by His Spirit I will be led.

The Wind of God is Moving

"O God, thou art my God; early will I seek thee: my soul thirsteth for thee, my flesh longeth for thee in a dry and thirsty land, where no water is."

Psalm 63:1

Some scholars say that this psalm was written by David to depict the intensity of his despair as he fled from his son, Absalom, who desired to kill him and take the kingdom (2 Samuel 15).

This time of shame, disgrace and disappointment forced David to assess his priorities. His greatest desire was to be on Mt. Zion in Jerusalem where he used to worship the Lord before the Ark of the Covenant.

This was the place of refreshing, healing and deliverance. He had now moved to a place of isolation and separation. This image of a "dry and thirsty land" creates the feeling of emptiness and barrenness, which implies alienation from the presence of God.

In times of loneliness, dryness, emptiness and despair, remember that praising God can turn your dry place into a watered garden.

Early Communion

Awaiting the sun and the onset of the dawn,
finds me on my knees reaching for life's keys.
Embracing my Maker with an empty mind allows
me to be saturated with principles divine.

God meets me early, before the day sets in.
I soar into His arms and draw comfort from
Him. My thoughts are exposed, my motives
checked and weighed. My emotions are not
paralyzed or open to the prey.

My decisions are based upon the Word of God.
He prints and writes them on the tables
of my heart. When I miss my encounter at the
start of the day, there lingers such an
emptiness that causes me to sway.

I need that time with Jesus — without
it I get unnerved. Communion and fellowship
causes me not to swerve. God, give me grace
to be consistent and never to allow my
flesh to be resistant. I need Your
refreshing early in the day. Please
keep calling me no matter how much
I stray.

Welcome, Morning Visitor!

"I love them that love me; and those that seek me early shall find me."
Proverbs 8:17

The Book of Proverbs is part of the Wisdom Books of the Bible. They offer us principles of life that encourage piety and respect for God's law.

This book is noted for its comparisons between opposites and the consequences of the application of these practices. Verse 17 highlights one of the devout and wise practices recommended by the writer: seeking the Lord early.

Seeking God early could mean before dawn or at dawn, or it could mean seeking Him earnestly above anything or anyone else.

Obedience brings great rewards. Wisdom speaks: "I love them," and "you will find me." Wisdom is ultimately found in the Lord. He will love those who love Him and will reveal Himself, freely give Himself and disclose His purpose to those who will seek (search) after Him over and beyond anything in their lives. What an incomparable reward.

The Inexplicable Purpose

Yes, I mean this. But no, I mean that.
Well, I thought I made it clear, but
sounds like I am chewing hay. Call
me what you will, or say I am a little
ill. I plead guilty to confusion and I
can't seem to find the solution.

I know what God said, although His promises
appear dead. I have nothing else to say, but
my faith will stand, I pray. God's purpose
will make a statement, even though my heart
is on the pavement.

Just give me some room, while I prepare
and let Him groom. I will say no more
because it seems as if I am not sure.
Please interpret my present
as being set up for the event.

The time is so near that this purpose
will be made clear. Laugh and mock
if you please, but God's will is coming
in with ease. No more comment,
just waiting for the advent.

His Purpose is Sure

"Then the word of the Lord came unto me, saying, Before I formed thee in the belly I knew thee; and before thou cameth forth out of the womb I sanctified thee, and I ordained thee a prophet unto the nations. Then said I, Ah, Lord God! behold, I cannot speak: for I am a child.

But the Lord said unto me, Say not, I am a child: for thou shalt go to all that I shall send thee, and whatsoever I command thee thou shalt speak."

Jeremiah 1:4-7

This passage describes Jeremiah's call to the prophetic office. During King Josiah's reign, in 629 B.C., Jeremiah was called while still a lad in Anathoth. Hilkiah, the high priest; Huldah, the prophetess and Zephaniah, the prophet, were also called. Jeremiah responded with words of insufficiency. He felt that he was a child (babe, boy) — inexperienced as a prophet and immature as a youth.

God responded by reproving him. While Jeremiah was in his mother's womb, God ordained and planned his purpose. He also consecrated and dedicated him to speak, pronounce and proclaim His word to the nation of Israel.

This record of Jeremiah's call encourages every struggling heart that attempts to execute the purpose of God amid feelings of insecurity and fear. God's word to us is the same as it was to Jeremiah. He chooses, ordains and dedicates earthen vessels to accomplish His heavenly purpose.

One's apparent deficiencies do not hamper the objective of God in the chosen one's life. Rise up and accept the fact that you were born for this, whatever "this" may be.

Glowing in the Dark

When all was well, before my world fell,
I fitted right in and things seemed to gel.
But now that I am in this dark place,
I am readily seen as a disgrace.

It is puzzling to the mind that
in this dimness, treasures I find.
I hardly noticed God's strength and His
grace until now. His love and mercy
has penetrated my cloud.

His brightness permeates the depth of my despair.
I arise with a glow that dispels all my fears.
The light of my countenance is very apparent.
It glitters as the gem of a diamond carat.

My sight is clear even in this unlit place.
All the time I complained was just a waste.
The gifts and skills, the beauty and the
shining, came from the face of the One
who brings radiant lighting.

This Light of Mine Has Pierced the Darkness

"Ye are the light of the world. A city that is set on an hill cannot be hid. Neither do men light a candle, and put it under a bushel, but on a candlestick; and it giveth light unto all that are in the house. Let your light so shine before men, that they may see your good works, and glorify your Father which is in heaven." Matthew 5:14-16

Matthew records the "Beatitudes," one of the most essential, foundational teachings of Jesus' ministry. It begins many of the sentences with the word "blessed," implying that if one obeys the commands and teachings, that one will be "blessed" or "happy."

You cannot live a submitted, obedient Christian life without enjoying spiritual and emotional benefits. If one is happy in pleasing and obeying Jesus, then one will glow with His light, power and presence as Moses did. After basking in the presence of God, Moses came down the mountain with a face so radiant that he had to veil it from others.

Whatever you receive from Jesus must be visible and luminous to others. This light must be so compelling that those in the world will notice the brilliance of your walk with God.

Spiritual Explosion

The quest for power and spiritual sight
has taken the world on a new flight.
Curious arts, New Agers, and psychics are
spreading their wings to invite the demonic.

Yet, we are not moved, deterred or surprised
because the power of God is resident in our lives.
The world seeks the force and the power of the
dark. The church is equipped to stop the
enemy's darts.

There is an explosion that is sweeping the
land. The dynamite of the Holy Ghost is
empowering His band. As the forces get
greater and spirits appear stronger, the
spirit-filled saints will rise with greater power.

We are pulling down strongholds and challenging
the fray. The battle is the Lord's and
their swords they must lay. Time to advance
and confront all the foes, for we are the
victors and the enemy is laden with woes.

Aim at the target and fire away. This is the end-time
explosion for which we have prayed.

Explosiveness in Him

"For the weapons of our warfare are not carnal, but mighty through God to the pulling down of strong holds." 2 Corinthians 10:4

The church at Corinth challenged the Apostle Paul's conversion, calling, commission and spiritual authority. He often handled them with a spirit of meekness and gentleness and did not exercise his apostolic authority in their presence. If they wandered from the Lord, however, he boldly chastised them through his letters.

The Corinthians judged Paul's actions based on their motive to get the apostle to respond in a fleshly manner. Paul reminded them that while he may walk or live in the flesh (in the human realm), he will not enter any confrontational situation with the military strategy of the flesh but with the mind of the Spirit.

The weapons (instruments) of our military attack are not on a carnal level, but are strong and powerful to the destroying or demolishing of the fortresses, citadels or bastions of the philosophies, learnings and eloquences of speech of the world.

The greatest battle is to bring into captivity all the thoughts and reasoning on which the flesh so strongly relies. The battle of the flesh and the carnal mind against the will and purpose of God can be defeated by our weapons of praise, prayer, fasting, Bible study and evangelism.

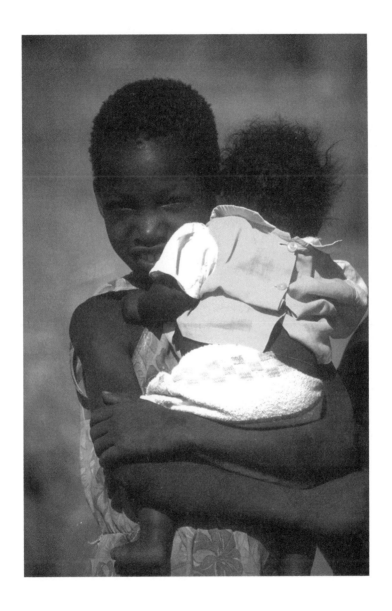

Holding the Promise

Is this a dream or an illusion? Pinch
or wake me out of this delusion.
Ah, but my eyes are open and alert.
There is no mistake, I can be blessed here
on earth.

I had resigned to live without this promise.
I just looked forward to my heavenly solace.
My God came when I least expected and showed me
love when I felt unprotected.

Many nights I prayed and imagined, "what if?"
I woke up the next day in brightness with a
new lift. I daydreamed of my future and gazed far
away, hoping to reach that very special day.

Time escaped, friends withdrew, boredom
set in and breakthroughs were small
and few. Then, surprisingly, my life took
a change. All that was promised came quickly
as the turning of a page.

My hands laid hold and my heart rejoiced.
My eyes beheld the glorious prize.
No, not a dream, not a figment of the mind.
It is an actual miracle and I am embracing
the divine.

A Faith Stroll

"Let us hold fast the profession of our faith without wavering; (for he is faithful that promised;)." Hebrews 10:23

The author of the Book of Hebrews wanted to protect the Jewish Christians from the danger of apostasy from Christ to Moses. This book includes a series of warnings in which this verse is contained.

The writer warns against letting go of one's faith. The believing Christian should hold fast (keep in mind, possess and seize) their faith (hope, confidence — which is faith exercised in reference to the future). This must be done without wavering (not leaning, without declension or deviation, firm).

This steadfastness of hope and belief is based on the character of God who makes the promise. Faithfulness (trustworthy and surety) is the characteristic most needed to uphold and fulfill covenants, agreements and promises.

The proof of His faithfulness is found throughout the Scriptures. Abraham and Sarah, Joseph, Rahab, Ruth and Naomi, Lazarus, Peter and Paul saw that He who promises is faithful. With this is mind, we can hope because God's tomorrow is better than today.

Closing All Doors

These outbursts of anger and moments
of rage can hardly be explained by the
reasons you gave. There are times
when we are loving, laughing and
playing, but suddenly, we turned and
monsters we were creating.

This is the time that we must
realize that our spirits are
being ravished and the enemy
is trying to leave us impoverished.
I am determined to break this awful spell
and to rebuke every evil spirit to the
pit of hell.

Mothers against fathers, children
fighting, too. This is the sign
that our home has lost its glue.
The power that binds us has been
weakened and broken. The presence
of God has been sought with a front
as a token.

Jesus is bigger than all the powers of
this world. He can destroy the evil
forces that hurl. They are powerless
when we give our heart unbridled. The
problem is, we have stood over the fence
and straddled.

I must say yes in spite of the cost.
I must be real even though friends I have
lost. I must not carry hate, shame or
pride. It is on their backs that the
enemy rides. I will check my spirit and
allow God to move within it.

When I obey Him the doors will be closed.
The spirits will fear me because of the
heavenly hosts. I sense my authority
to loose and to bind. I will stop crying
and strengthen my mind. You check your spirit
and I will do the same, then we will see the
deliverance in Jesus' Name.

No Place for Demons

"Then he called his twelve disciples together, and gave them power and authority over all devils, and to cure diseases." Luke 9:1

This passage characterizes the call of the twelve disciples to the ministry. Inherent in the commission is the power, authority or right to do incredible and supernatural works.

Jesus bestowed upon them supernatural power and authority over devils. They were empowered by the One who has all power in His hands. This literally means Jesus gave them force and ability, jurisdiction and privilege over all demonic beings or presence. They also healed sicknesses and diseases.

This power is not limited to the Twelve but is available to all who are filled with the Holy Spirit. Acts 1:8 boldly states, "But ye shall receive power . . ." That's the same power, the same Lord and the same results over demons, adversaries and circumstances.

Release the power in you and demons will become subject to the authority of the Lord Jesus Christ.

Counting the Costs

I am good at saving pennies.
I am better at holding grudges.
I can even remember when my sister
took my fudgies. This ability to
recall all the bad times and the
falls has made me hard and callous,
and hung my dreams on the gallows.

Why am I so prone to be attached to the
negative and forget His goodness
and His benefit? The times that
I got hurt, the hours of heart
throbbing pain, are so vivid in my
mind and no positive release I gain.

Then trouble flooded my life, and my home
became the residence of strife.
I almost lost everything, and destruction
took on wings. A blast of truth
hit me, and I quickly realized
there are more things for which to give thanks
and that I did more than just survived.

I looked at the health and strength
that God has freely given. I imbibed
in His grace and mercy every morning
I'd risen. I looked in the cupboard
and saw no empty shelf. I looked at
my children and assessed my future
wealth.

It is time to reevaluate my blessings
and my graces. I need to bow down
and give thanks for all my places.
I denounce every thought of anger
and woe. I raise my hands to Jesus
who has conquered every foe.

He did not have to keep me in all
of my ways. He did not have
to show me how to escape the traps
and sways. He guarded my spirit
even when I could not see. I am
humbled that the Master keeps
remembering me.

Blessings Innumerable

"It is of the Lord's mercies that we are not consumed, because his compassions fail not. They are new every morning: great is thy faithfulness."
Lamentations 3:22,23

Jeremiah, an Old Testament prophet who had a distinctive call on his life from his mother's womb, found himself in prison because he spoke out for God.

Yes, it is possible to be persecuted, rejected, incarcerated and killed for the sake of the Gospel. It is very human to complain as a "suffering servant" in times of distress. The complaint in this passage is an "elegy," which means sorrowing, bemoaning or bewailing a difficult situation.

After Jeremiah moaned and murmured for a while, he looked at the other side of his situation and made a great discovery. God was faithful (steadfast) every morning and issued new mercies and compassion. Jeremiah stopped complaining and counted the cost. He discovered that even in the worst of times, God was consistent in His care and provision.

Remembering God's mercy is more peaceful, rewarding and therapeutic than concentrating on the negatives of our existence. Jesus will never abandon us.

Gifted and Whole

I am gifted and blessed with
God's grace and holiness. This
deposit illumines my mind and
I create with freedom sublime.

It is not just inspiration alone,
but a relationship that flows
from the throne. I am not being
used and refused, but I am growing
in the Gospel of Good News.

There are many who are talented
and bright but live narrow and
see with short sight. They can
only excel with their gift-mix,
but they cannot deal with
life and its tricks.

Love is not present with all of
their talent. Peace is not
reigning with all of their training.
It is a pity for them to bless so many
but walk away empty and act real
funny.

I found a place where joy abounds.
It is different than the limelight
and the crowds. After I use the
favor and flair, I come away with
the Master who cares.

This relationship is second to none.
It gives me the grace to be tempered
and to overcome. I pray that this
balance will keep my soul from
craving stardom and earthly gold.

This is just a reminder to all who
read. Keep Jesus in front and let
Him masterfully lead. All that we
have came from above. Let's keep
things in place and walk in His love.

Tempered in Him

"Yea doubtless, and I count all things but loss for the excellency of the knowledge of Christ Jesus my Lord: for whom I have suffered the loss of all things, and do count them but dung, that I may win Christ."

Philippians 3:8

Paul, a citizen of Tarsus and of Rome, came from a Jewish heritage and called himself "a Hebrew of the Hebrews" (Philippians 3:5).

An outstanding scholar of Jewish Law, Paul attended the school of Hillel and "sat at the feet of Gamaliel," the greatest rabbi of his day. Paul became a great missionary, evangelist, preacher, teacher and author of much of the New Testament. Yet, he put his relationship with the Lord above everything that he had learned or experienced.

This multi-talented, multifaceted, creative and anointed gift to the early church expressed his priority in life. He actually counted (deemed, considered) all things —everything he was or had — but a mere loss (damage, inferior) for the excellency (superiority) of the knowledge (experiential understanding) of Christ (the Shinning One) Jesus (Savior, Healer) his Lord (Boss): for whom he had suffered (experienced damage or loss) of all things (things from his former life that he valued), and he counts them as dung (garbage, what is thrown to the dogs) that he may win (gain) Christ.

This statement challenges us to place all that is dear at the bottom of the list and value an intimate, personal relationship with the Lord, who is the giver of all gifts and blessings.

Lightheartedness

Flowers, hugs, kisses and touches
sweep over my thoughts with laughter
and wishes.

It is rare and less often I can relish
the good, enjoy the pleasant and express
joy as I should.

Hold and nurse the precious sweet
times. For he who hates us snatches
and defiles.

Inhale the peace, rediscover God's love.
Close your eyes and hear melodies
from above.

Separate from the lies and the garbage,
the ado and drama, the hustle and the
excess baggage.

Fret nor fear, just slide easily through
this day. Clear away the cobwebs and
like David, just play.

Enjoy Him! Adore Him! Embrace Him!
Love Him! Jesus comes to make your heart merry
and give comfort to the dreary and the weary.

A Cheerful Spirit

"Speaking to yourselves in psalms and hymns and spiritual songs, singing and making melody in your heart to the Lord." Ephesians 5:19

Paul's exhortation to the church of Ephesus can be fully applied to our lives today. He stressed the need to love, to avoid lustful communication and activities, to walk orderly before the Lord and to be filled with the Spirit. Then he mentioned this key verse: to sing and make melody to the Lord in the heart.

Lightheartedness to the Christian is different than that of the world. The world uses lust and carnal pleasure to keep itself happy. Yet, they enjoy this cheerfulness for only a short time. The music stops playing, the hangover sets in and the friends leave. Only the Christian experiences true freedom and lightness of spirit.

This verse tells us how to sustain this wholesome attitude. First, we must be filled with the Spirit. The word means to be fully empowered, inspired and saturated with His Spirit. If we do not keep this fervent, spiritual disposition, we will not enjoy the delightful liberty that brings peace and joy to one's heart.

Paul admonishes us to continually speak (talk, utter, say) to ourselves (self-talk) in psalms (words put to music), hymns (songs of celebration of God) and spiritual songs (religious or anointed songs). We need to make melody (play an instrument or listen to a piece played on an instrument, which glorifies God) in our hearts or minds unto the Lord.

The world is filled with distractions, especially in the area of music. Some music gives us the blues; another kind stirs up lust; others open us up to demonic activity. The Spirit of God guards our hearts and minds as we fill them continually with songs, music and melody that glorify God. In turn, we will have a pleasant, cheerful, delightful and positive spirit in the midst of a cruel and perplexing world.

Sing unto the Lord a new song. Sing!

Seed Planter

Fingernails dirty, cuticles broken and
red. Digging and plowing and shaping
flower beds describe a side of life
that demands extra care. Most people
can't be bothered and never indulge,
I fear.

This act of seed planting requires
sacrifice, discomfort, pressure or price.
But the returns are consistent with the
fulfillment of the act. God guarantees a harvest.
It's just part of the pact.

The reaping will not come the same
day of the planting. The gains will not
surface while the sower is watering.
But the season of rewards will come in
due time. No one has given and did not
strike a gold mine.

Release inner and outer splendor
and qualities that will make life
full with grandeur. Ignite fires,
calm fears, extend an arm and
give a listening ear. These are
bread cast upon the water, which
will yield proceeds with joys
and spirits with laughter.

The Cycle of Giving

"Cast thy bread upon the waters: for thou shalt find it after many days."
Ecclesiastes 11:1

God gave King Solomon wisdom above all the men who ever lived. Solomon's reign, administration and writings demonstrated this priceless gift. In this poetic book of the Bible, which contrasts good and evil and deals with the inexplicable injustices of life, it is not surprising that Solomon touches on giving and the challenges associated with it.

Life is filled with uncertainties. As a result, we attempt to build into our sphere certainties and securities that assure us of success. This command to "cast thy bread upon the waters" must be understood within its cultural and geographical setting to fully comprehend it.

What was their custom for sowing seed? Farmers cast the seeds from their boats in the overflowing waters of the Nile or the swampy ground. After the waters receded, the seed in the flooded area would spring up and grow (Isaiah 32:20). This soil, rich with minerals, was conducive to growth and nurturing of the seed.

This verse could also allude to the sower who takes a portion of the bread-corn from his harvest, which means he deducts from his family what they could eat. This is not robbery but wisdom because he uses this portion to sow the next year's harvest. He also gives a portion to the poor, who cannot pay him back in any way. This investment appears to yield no apparent returns.

The wise man, however, challenges us to cast in the flowing waters that seemingly would wash the seed away and not allow it to grow, or to give to someone who will never be able to return the favor. Even though it appears to be a risk and a dare, Scripture states that not many days hence it will return. The waters of the Nile will recede and the rich soil will suck in the seed, causing it to produce fruit.

There is no way to know if this really works other than to do it. Take the risk and sow even if no reward is apparent.

Something Better

Someone is always trying to set my
limits, telling me things will not change
and to settle with it.

Life must be different with Jesus at the
head. I keep saying those words as
I toss on my bed.

I reject the system of the world and
its mores, its poisonous darts that
corrupt in so many ways.

Whenever I pray, new discoveries I find.
The Holy Spirit implants possibilities
in my mind.

I can't settle for the little and
make do. I know I am not the majority
but among the very few.

The shout and churchy dance is all
that some desire. But way down
in my soul, I am consumed with a
spiritual fire.

The fire generates excellence, virtue,
godly pride, power and passion.
A quiet resolve without form or fashion.

Keep your mediocrity and popularity.
I will strive for the better and satisfy
my spiritual curiosity.

Viewing the Best

"The thief cometh not, but for to steal, and to kill, and to destroy: I am come that they might have life, and that they might have it more abundantly."
John 10:10

The Pharisees (religious leaders of Jesus' time) opposed Jesus and His teaching, especially His claim to be Messiah and King. Considering themselves the true leaders of the people, they thought that Jesus was an imposter.

Jesus, therefore, gave this discourse on the sheep and the shepherd. He boldly proclaimed that He was the door to the sheepfold and that no one can enter the Kingdom of God except through Him. Not all the sheep (people) will respond to Him — only the ones that the Father gives Him.

Jesus also shared the benefits of being in His fold and under His watchful eye. The Good Shepherd cares for the sheep and protects them from the thief.

Thieves and robbers represented those from the old tradition who did not have the people's best interest at heart. Jesus, however, came to give them something better. The thief (robber) comes to steal (swindle), kill (slay, slaughter, blow upon or sacrifice by fire), and destroy (to cause to perish or crush to powder). Jesus came that we may have life (quicken with life-giving power and force, not just to protect, but to impart to us) and that more abundantly (highly, beyond measure, superfluously).

This kind of life is worth embracing. We should be comforted in our hearts that each day the Lord guarantees a better experience, home, position, relationship and future. The best is yet to come!

Courage to Live

Awakened by the notion that life is passing by,
I took a closer look at time and kept asking why?
Why I took the paths I trod? Why I ran from
corrective rods? Why I dodged, hemmed and hawed
at the things that seem too hard?

The challenges, the risks and the dares filled my
heart with anxiety and my mind with fears. It
took more than half of my existence to realize that
life comes with much resistance.

I now release my apprehensions and through worship
and praise I yield my tensions. The everlasting
life of Christ guides me on this journey, but not
without praise to His glory.

I will be bold, I will be strong. Living is doing
no matter how hard or long. The victory is in knowing
that I tried my best, and that the Holy Ghost empowered
me for every test.

Because He Lives, I Live

"I am crucified with Christ: nevertheless I live; yet not I, but Christ liveth in me: and the life which I now live in the flesh I live by the faith of the Son of God, who loved me, and gave himself for me." Galatians 2:20

The Galatian churches existed because the Apostle Paul preached, labored and established the work of the Lord in that area. They were the result of his apostleship and his missionary endeavors.

These churches had become the target of the legalistic teachings of the Jewish Christians, who wanted to impose circumcision and some aspects of their ceremonial laws as a requirement for salvation.

Paul wrote this epistle to fight against the Judaizers' determination to manipulate his teachings to the Galatians. The first two chapters were written in defense of his apostleship, which leads us to this verse.

The Law had benefited Paul. This very Law had made him aware of his sin and led him to Christ. This Law was the basis for Jesus' crucifixion and man's redemption, which provided a different kind of life for those who come to God.

The perfect tense of this word "crucified" means that the propitious death on the cross still has present and continuing effects on the believers' life. The dying out of the flesh and worldly life-style was and is being subdued, overpowered and executed by the life of Christ. This life, also, quickens and imparts the eternal life as Christ dwells within the Christian.

Legal obedience to the Law has now been replaced by the new life of Christ through the faith of the redeemed. This marvelous paradox of dying to live can only be experienced as we surrender to the eternal life of Jesus Christ.

Learning to Listen

I've watched your lips moving, muttering, and
speaking. Yet, I seldom perceived your heart or the
message you were releasing. This habit to look but not
to hear is a part of a relationship without care.

In my prayers I tend to talk profusely. I try my best
to listen, but sometimes I move too hurriedly. One day
I took the time to wait before God's presence. Oh, what
a joy I found and peace to quiet all turbulence.

It is a secret place where quietness is needed. It is
a time to listen and wisdom must be heeded. I had to
calm myself, relax myself and still my uneasy spirit.

My ears became my antennae until I heard clearly from
heaven. These messages were filled with precious
thoughts that no human could have given.

The Power to Hear

"Therefore whosoever heareth these sayings of mine, and doeth them, I will liken him unto a wise man, which built his house upon a rock."
                                            Matthew 7:24

Jesus accomplished His mission on earth by teaching the principles of His Kingdom. The Sermon on the Mount (Matt. 5-7) and the Beatitudes (Matt. 5:2-12) encouraged His hearers to become morally and spiritually matured disciples. He used various methods of teachings, especially parables, to influence His hearers to become doers of the Word.

Jesus used the example of wise and foolish builders to make a point about true discipleship. We are challenged to build our lives upon the teachings of Jesus Christ. If we do, we will be like the wise builder who chose a solid foundation for his home. The rock alluded to the immovable character of our Lord.

The words of Christ are the foundational truths that keep us from defeat and destruction in the time of calamity (rain, flood, wind). Hearing the Word is not limited to listening and intellectualizing the Word. Obeying the Word is the key to secure, safe and sound living.

Because our lives are laden with uncertainties, Christians must become true disciples of the Lord Jesus Christ by "doing the Book."

Subject/Scripture Index

Praises for Daily Moments with God

Through the insightfulness of these daily meditations, your spiritual life will be challenged and guided along the path of God's truth and love.

Professor Gail Ann Hightower
Bassoonist, Producer, President of Universal Symphony
Queens, New York

Jackie McCullough bears her heart in this intriguing collection of poetry and prose. It is an exposé of the soul of a woman whose walk with God has been as intense as it has been collaborative. This Caribbean woman has a heart for women of all nations and races. To read her work is to peer into her own relationship and "embrace" with The Divine and to "faith stroll" with the Father. It is a book which is both useful and provocative and which would be a companion for the busy yet thoughtful reader.

Dr. Patricia Morgan
Professor at Oral Roberts University
Author of The Battle for the Seed
Tulsa, Oklahoma

Like a flowing stream that refreshes you during times of thirst, these inspired writings will lift your spirit to a place of quietness and lead your soul down paths of confidence and strength.

Dr. Caroline D. Showell
Evangelist, President of Transformed, Inc.
Baltimore, Maryland

as good as or better than you are. Within each of us lies the potential to be an effective leader. *Becoming A Leader* uncovers the secrets of dynamic leadership that will show you how to be a leader in your family, school, community, church and job. No matter where you are or what you do in life this book can help you to inevitably become a leader. Remember: it is never too late to become a leader. As in every tree there is a forest, so in every follower there is a leader.

The African Cultural Heritage Topical Bible

The African Cultural Heritage Topical Bible is a quick and convenient reference Bible. It has been designed for use in personal devotions as well as group Bible studies. It's the newest and most complete reference Bible designed to reveal the Black presence in the Bible and highlight the contributions and exploits of Blacks from the past to present. It's a great tool for students, clergy, teachers — practically anyone seeking to learn more about the Black presence in Scripture, but didn't know where to start.

The African Cultural Heritage Topical Bible contains:
• Over 395 easy to find **topics**
• **3,840 verses** that are systematically organized
• A comprehensive listing of Black Inventions
• Over **150 pages** of Christian Afrocentric articles on Blacks in the Bible, Contributions of Africa, African Foundations of Christianity, Culture, Identity, Leadership and Racial Reconciliation written by Myles Munroe, Wayne Perryman, Dr. Leonard Lovett, Dr. Trevor L. Grizzle, James Giles and Mensa Otabil.
Available in KJV and NIV versions

The God Factor

by James Giles

Is something missing in your life? Do you find yourself at the mercy of your circumstances? Is your self-esteem at an all-time low? Are your dreams only a faded memory? You could be missing the one element that could make the difference between success and failure, poverty and prosperity, and creativity and apathy. Knowing God supplies the creative genius you need to reach your potential and realize your dream. You'll be challenged as James Giles shows you how to tap into your God-given genius, take steps toward reaching your goal, pray big and get answers, eat right and stay healthy, prosper economically and personally, and leave a lasting legacy for your children.

Making the Most of Your Teenage Years

by David Burrows

Most teenagers live for today. Living only for today, however, can kill you. When teenagers have no plan for their future, they follow a plan that someone else devised. Unfortunately, this plan often leads them to drugs, sex, crime, jail and early death. How can you make the most of your teenage years? Discover who you really are – and how to plan for the three phases of your life. You can develop your skill, achieve your dreams and still have fun.

The Biblical Principles of Success

by Arthur L. Mackey Jr.

There are only three types of people in the world: people who make things happen, people who watch things happen and people who do not know what in the world is happening. *The Biblical Principles of Success* will help you become one who makes things happen. Success is not a matter of "doing it my way." It is turning from a personal, selfish philosophy to God's outreaching, sharing way of life. This powerful book teaches you how to tap into success principles that are guaranteed – *the Biblical principles of success!*

Flaming Sword
by Tai Ikomi
Scripture memorization and meditation bring tremendous spiritual power, however many Christians find it to be an uphill task. Committing Scriptures to memory will transform the mediocre Christian to a spiritual giant. This book will help you to become addicted to the powerful practice of Scripture memorization and help you obtain the victory that you desire in every area of your life. *Flaming Sword* is your pathway to spiritual growth and a more intimate relationship with God.

Beyond the Rivers of Ethiopia
by Mensa Otabil
Beyond the Rivers of Ethiopia is a powerful and revealing look into God's purpose for the Black race. It gives scholastic yet simple answers to questions you have always had about the Black presence in the Bible. At the heart of this book is a challenge and call to the offspring of the Children of Africa, both on the continent and throughout the world, to come to grips with their true identity as they go *Beyond the Rivers of Ethiopia.*

Single Life
by Earl D. Johnson
A book that candidly addresses the spiritual and physical dimensions of the single life is finally here. *Single Life* shows the reader how to make their singleness a celebration rather than a burden. This positive approach to singles uses enlightening examples from Apostle Paul, himself a single, to beautifully portray the dynamic aspects of the single life by serving the Lord more effectively. The book gives fresh insight on practical issues such as coping with sexual desires, loneliness and preparation for your future mate. Written in a lively style, the author admonishes singles to seek first the kingdom of God and rest assured in God's promise to supply their needs... including a life partner!

Available at your local bookstore
or by contacting:

Pneuma Life Publishing
P.O. Box 1127
Rockville, MD 20849

1-800-727-3218